HORSES

The MORGAN Horse

by Sarah Maass

Capstone press

Mankato, Minnesota

Edge Books are published by Capstone Press,
151 Good Counsel Drive, P.O. Box 669, Mankato, Minnesota 56002.
www.capstonepress.com

Library of Congress Cataloging-in-Publication Data
Maass, Sarah.
    The Morgan horse / by Sarah Maass.
    p. cm.—(Edge books. Horses)
    Includes bibliographical references and index.
    ISBN 0-7368-3767-1 (hardcover)
    1. Morgan horse—Juvenile literature. I. Title. II. Series.
SF293.M8M24 2005
636.1'77—dc22   2004019415

Summary: Describes the Morgan horse, including its history, physical features, and
uses today.

Editorial Credits
Carrie A. Braulick, editor; Juliette Peters, designer; Deirdre Barton, photo researcher;
    Scott Thoms, photo editor

Photo Credits
Artville, LLC, 7
Bruce Coleman Inc./Nicholas Conte, 29
Capstone Press/Gary Sundermeyer (objects), 21, 26
Courtesy of the American Morgan Horse Association Inc., 12, 15, 20, 25
Courtesy of Heidi Kunkel (owner)/Bob Moseder (photographer), 27
Courtesy of the National Museum of the Morgan Horse, 5
Lombard Antiquarian Maps and Prints, 9
© 2004 Mark J. Barrett, front cover, back cover, 6, 14, 16–17
Paige DD Singer, 19
Timothy Johnson, 11, 22, 23

**Capstone Press thanks Kathy Newcomb, member, American Morgan Horse
Association (AMHA) Board of Directors, for her assistance in preparing this book.**

1 2 3 4 5 6 10 09 08 07 06 05

Table of Contents

Chapter 1: One Horse, Many Admirers....... 4

Chapter 2: Strong and Stylish................... 10

Chapter 3: Built for Combined Driving 18

Chapter 4: Morgans in Action 24

FEATURES

Photo Diagram 16

Fast Facts 28

Glossary.. 30

Read More... 31

Internet Sites 31

Index 32

One Horse, Many Admirers

In the late 1700s, Americans worked hard to make their new country grow. They cleared forests to build homes and plant crops. The settlers expected their horses to work hard as well. They used horses to move rocks and logs from forests.

Around 1791, a horse in Vermont named Figure helped clear forests. People were impressed by the small horse's strength. Figure and his offspring were the first Morgan horses.

Today, Morgans are still known for their strength. Morgans pull carriages in driving competitions. Morgans also are known for their beauty and cooperative personalities.

Learn about:
- ★ Figure
- ★ Driving horses
- ★ Morgans in the Civil War

Figure started the Morgan breed. He was known for his strength and beauty.

The First Morgan

In the early 1790s, teacher Justin Morgan owned Figure. Robert Evans lived near Morgan. Evans needed a horse to move logs from forests. Morgan let Evans use Figure.

Figure could pull more weight than many larger horses. One day, Evans and Figure met a small crowd gathered around a large log. The log needed to be pulled to a nearby sawmill. Several large horses tried to pull it, but they could hardly move it. Evans said Figure could pull the log. The crowd laughed at this idea. But they were amazed after Figure reached the mill with the log.

The Start of the Breed

Figure's qualities made him popular. People liked Figure for his strength, speed, and appearance. Figure's upright neck made him look proud. He had a sleek coat. Figure's sturdy body was slender instead of bulky.

Many people wanted to have horses with Figure's features. They bred, or mated, their mares with Figure. Figure's foals were almost always very much like him.

In 1798, Morgan died. People began calling Figure "Justin Morgan" after his owner. They called Figure's descendants Morgans.

Morgans in the 1800s

In the 1800s, Morgans became popular driving horses. They pulled farm machinery in fields. They also pulled people in buggies and carriages.

As harness racing became popular, Morgans showed that they could pull carts at record speeds. Morgans Black Hawk and Ethan Allen were famous harness racing horses.

During the Civil War (1861–1865), soldiers rode Morgans and used them to pull cannons. Morgans obeyed their masters even as gunshots and cannon fire rang out. The First Vermont Cavalry rode only Morgans.

The AMHA

In 1909, Morgan owners in the United States formed the Morgan Horse Club. In 1971, the club's name changed to the American Morgan Horse Association (AMHA). The AMHA keeps records of each registered horse's ancestry. Today, about 147,000 Morgans are registered with the AMHA.

Ethan Allen won 33 races during his 16-year racing career.

Chapter 2

Strong and Stylish

Today's Morgans still look like Figure. They also share Figure's gentle, cooperative personality.

Colors

Many Morgans are bay, brown, or chestnut. Bay horses are red-brown with black manes and tails. Chestnut horses are a copper color. Black, gray, cream, dun, palomino, and buckskin are other Morgan colors. Dun horses usually are yellow-brown. They have a black stripe down the middle of their backs. Palomino horses are tan with blond manes and tails. Buckskin horses are tan with black manes and tails. Many Morgans have white face and leg markings.

Learn about:
- ☆ **Morgan colors**
- ☆ **Personality**
- ☆ **Gaited Morgans**

Morgans can be one of many colors, including black.

Morgans have large nostrils and expressive eyes.

Main Features

Several features make the Morgan easy to recognize. It has a short head with a wide forehead. The Morgan has large eyes and nostrils. The horse's arched, muscular neck narrows as it meets the head. A long, thick mane and tail are common. The Morgan's short, strong back and sturdy legs help it pull heavy loads.

Horses are measured from the ground to the withers, or top of the shoulders. Most Morgans stand 14.1 to 15.2 hands high. A hand is equal to 4 inches (10 centimeters). Morgans are smaller than many other horses. Thoroughbreds, Quarter Horses, and other breeds often are at least 15 hands tall.

Morgans carry their heads high as they move.

Personality

Morgans are known for their cooperative personalities. They usually are willing to work for long periods of time without becoming stubborn. This feature makes them good horses for long races and trail rides.

Morgans also are intelligent and gentle. People usually can train them easily and trust them around children.

Movement

Morgans move gracefully. They step high. Morgans also carry their heads and tails higher than most other horses do.

A few Morgans are gaited. Most horses naturally can do four gaits. These gaits are the walk, trot, canter, and gallop.

Gaited horses can perform an extra gait. This gait is usually called a single-foot. A horse performing the single-foot sometimes has only one foot on the ground.

Parking Out

For some classes at horse shows, Morgans are trained to stand in a "parked out" position. They stand with their front legs straight down and their back legs stretched out behind them. This position shows off the horses' features.

Parking out began in the 1800s. At the time, women often wore long skirts. It was easier for a woman to get on a horse when it was parked out.

Long, thick mane

Large eyes

Upright neck

High, strong shoulders

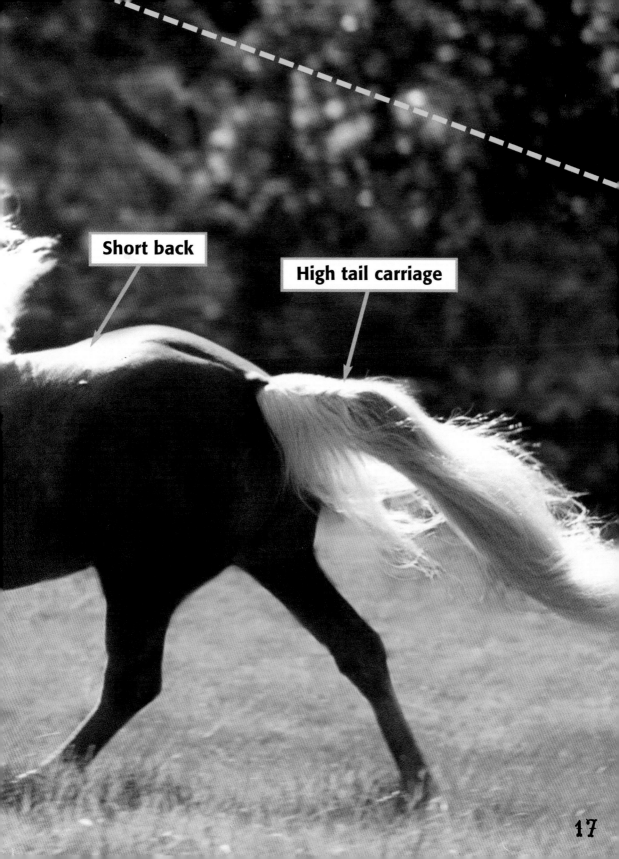

Short back

High tail carriage

17

Chapter 3

Built for Combined Driving

Most people no longer use horses and carriages to travel. But driving is still one of the Morgan's most common uses. Morgans compete in more driving events than any other breed.

Combined Driving

Many Morgans compete in combined driving events. These events have three parts. Sometimes, each part is on a different day. Other events last only one or two days.

Learn about:
- ★ **Combined driving events**
- ★ **Dressage**
- ★ **Ground driving**

Morgans sometimes cross water in combined driving competitions.

Drivers complete the dressage test in the first part of a combined driving event. This test shows how well drivers communicate with their horses. Drivers must memorize and complete a pattern. The horses walk, trot, and back up.

Drivers must judge their distance from objects in the cones course.

The second part of a combined driving event is the marathon. Drivers guide their horses through a series of obstacles. The horses might have to go through water or a maze of fences. The horses also may need to make tight turns around trees or travel through narrow openings.

Horses must be in good physical condition for the marathon test. The course usually covers 5 to 13 miles (8 to 21 kilometers). Veterinarians check the horses during the marathon to make sure the horses aren't too tired.

The third part of a combined driving event is the cones course. Drivers guide their horses through pairs of numbered cones. Tennis balls are on top of the cones. The winning driver moves through the course the fastest without knocking balls off the cones.

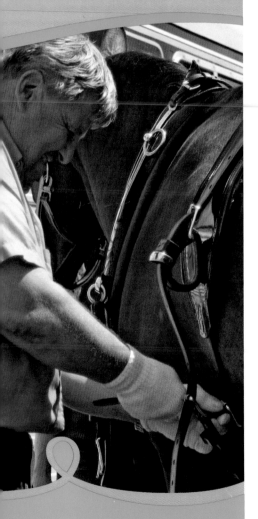

People training a driving horse should make sure the harness fits the horse well.

Training for Driving

Many people train their Morgans to drive when the horses are 2 or 3 years old. Fitting a horse with a bridle and a harness are the first steps. A bridle has straps that fit around the horse's head. The straps connect to a metal mouthpiece called a bit. Straps called reins connect to the bit. A harness includes straps for connecting a cart to a horse.

Ground driving helps horses become used to moving in a harness. The handler walks far behind the horse and holds onto long reins. The handler teaches the horse to turn by gently pulling on one rein. Ground driving is also called long-lining.

Next, the horse learns to pull an empty two-wheeled cart. When a horse is first hitched to a cart, many handlers have another person walk beside the horse. This person helps guide the horse and keep it calm. Later, the driver guides the horse from the cart.

Some experienced driving horses pull carriages with another horse. Two horses hitched side by side to one carriage are known as a pair.

Ground driving helps a horse become used to a person guiding it from behind.

Chapter 4

Morgans in Action

People who enjoy the thrill of competing with their Morgans have many opportunities to show off their skills. Most combined driving competitions are held in the eastern United States. Canada, Mexico, and some European countries also have combined driving events. Top combined driving teams compete in the Triple Crown of Combined Driving and the U.S. National Championships.

Learn about:
- ☆ Major driving competitions
- ☆ Morgan horse shows
- ☆ Horse care

Horse shows have classes for children as well as adults.

Horses with Many Talents

Some people compete at Morgan shows that are approved by the United States Equestrian Federation (USEF). Competitors in these shows can enter several events, or classes. Both riding and driving classes are held. Participants in USEF-approved shows may qualify for the Grand National and World Championship Morgan Horse Show. This show takes place in Oklahoma each October.

Morgans are becoming more popular as dressage horses. Dressage riders train their horses to complete a set of advanced moves. The Morgan Dressage Association helps promote the use of Morgans in the sport.

Owning a Morgan

Owning a Morgan is a big responsibility. Morgans need a great deal of care. Chores include feeding, cleaning out stalls, and brushing. Morgans also need large spaces to exercise. Most

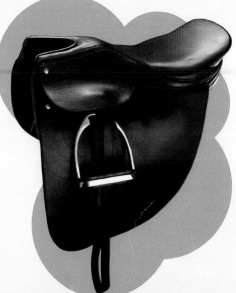

horses live 25 to 30 years. With good care, Morgans may live a few years longer than other breeds.

The story of how one horse formed a new breed continues to attract people to Morgans. No one knows the exact ancestry of Figure. But no one will ever forget him as they look at today's graceful, talented Morgans.

HVK Courageous Flaire

The Morgan stallion HVK Courageous Flaire has become famous as a driving and English performance horse. In 1991, 1993, and 1997, he was world champion in a driving class called park harness. In 1995, 1999, and 2000, he was world champion in an English riding class called park saddle. HVK Courageous Flaire also has three offspring that have won world championships.

Fast Facts:
The Morgan Horse

Name: Morgans are named after Justin Morgan. In the 1790s, Morgan owned a horse named Figure in Vermont. Figure started the Morgan breed.

History: In 1789, the first Morgan horse was born in the United States. People called the horse Figure. Later, they called him Justin Morgan. All Morgans are descendants of this horse.

Height: Morgans are 14.1 to 15.2 hands (about 5 feet or 1.5 meters) tall at the withers. Each hand equals 4 inches (10 centimeters).

Weight: 900 to 1,200 pounds (400 to 540 kilograms)

Colors: bay, brown, chestnut, black, gray, palomino, cream, dun, buckskin

Features: short back; high, strong shoulders; thick mane and tail; muscular, arched neck; short head; wide forehead; large eyes; high tail carriage

Personality: intelligent, gentle, cooperative

Abilities: Morgans make excellent driving horses. They pull buggies, carriages, and sleighs. They also make good show and trail riding horses.

Life span: about 25 to 30 years

Glossary

bit (BIT)—the metal mouthpiece of the bridle

bridle (BRYE-duhl)—the straps that fit around a horse's head and connect to a bit to control a horse while riding and driving

dressage (druh-SAHJ)—a riding or driving style in which horses complete a pattern while doing advanced moves

gait (GATE)—the manner in which a horse moves; gaits include the walk, trot, canter, and gallop.

harness (HAR-niss)—a set of leather straps and metal pieces that connect a horse to a plow, cart, or wagon

mare (MAIR)—an adult female horse

qualify (KWAHL-uh-fye)—to be allowed to compete in an event

single-foot (SING-guhl-FUHT)—a gait in which the horse sometimes has only one foot on the ground

stallion (STAL-yuhn)—an adult male horse that can be used for breeding

Read More

Barnes, Julia. *101 Facts about Horses and Ponies.* 101 Facts about Pets. Milwaukee: Gareth Stevens, 2002.

Lomberg, Michelle. *Caring for Your Horse.* Caring for Your Pet. New York: Weigl Publishers, 2004.

Ransford, Sandy. *Horse and Pony Encyclopedia.* New York: Kingfisher, 2004.

Internet Sites

FactHound offers a safe, fun way to find Internet sites related to this book. All of the sites on FactHound have been researched by our staff.

Here's how:

1. Visit *www.facthound.com*
2. Type in this special code **0736837671** for age-appropriate sites. Or enter a search word related to this book for a more general search.
3. Click on the **Fetch It** button.

FactHound will fetch the best sites for you!

Index

American Morgan Horse
    Association (AMHA), 8
appearance, 7, 10, 13

bit, 22
breed registry. See American
    Morgan Horse Association
    (AMHA)
bridle, 22

care, 26–27
Civil War, 8
colors, 10
combined driving events, 18,
    20–21
    Triple Crown of Combined
        Driving, 24
    U.S. National Championships,
        24

dressage, 20, 26

Evans, Robert, 6, 7

Figure, 4, 6–7, 10, 27

gaits, 14–15
Grand National and World
    Championship Morgan Horse
    Show, 26
ground driving, 22

harness racing, 8
HVK Courageous Flaire, 27

Morgan Dressage Association, 26
Morgan, Justin, 6, 7
movement, 14–15

pair, 23
parking out, 15
personality, 4, 10, 14

reins, 22

size, 13

training, 22–23

United States Equestrian
    Federation (USEF), 26